Inspiring Stories

for

Amazing Boys

D1715246

Children's Stories About

Things That Matters

Maggie Bell

Table of Contents

Introduction

ey, little boy! Do You Know There's Something Very Precious Inside of You?

I'm talking about the little spark of your uniqueness!

See, within yourself, there's a little spark that can allow you to do great things, accomplish fantastic results, and achieve ambitious goals... all right inside of you!

1

But you must preserve it, treat it well and protect it because it will help you every time you could fall.

Maybe you won't fall or maybe you will...that's ok, cause we all fall!

Sometimes you could think you won't be good enough, that you won't deserve something, or you'll doubt yourself... Well, your spark will be there to remind you how special you are!

Just as the protagonists of the stories in this book.

Indeed, you'll see how boys just like you have overcome their fears by working on their self-esteem, reached the top of the mountain by feeding the flame of their courage, and developed meaningful self-acceptance by extinguishing the voices of those who judged them.

These short stories will help you for:

- Developing self-esteem, becoming more confident, and always Having courage;

- Enhancing the friendship value and protecting the gift of kindness;

- Forge your personality with inner-strength and create a perseverance attitude;

Remember them whenever:

- Someone will make fun of you for who you are or what you do (you're unique, you're special, always remember that!)

- You'll face a difficult time like a bad grade at school or an embarrassing moment during a match game of your favorite sport;

- Or when you might be disappointed by something you hoped would be better (don't be afraid to fail, it's just an attempt!)

You're perfect just the way you are, and you'll make great things!

The Backyard Monster

Once upon a time, there was a boy named Cameron. Cameron lived in a big blue house with his mom, dad, and little sister, Josie. Cameron loved to play outside. He enjoyed helping his mom garden, helping his sister with art activities, and catching bugs was his favorite.

One day, Cameron and Josie were playing in the backyard with their toy shovels. They were building dirt castles so all the bugs they caught could play and roam around. It was their favorite thing to do together.

As they were playing, Cameron hearts a loud scary noise from behind the backyard gate.

"GRRRRRRR..." it buzzed loudly.

"A monster! It's a monster!" Josie said, afraid. She ran inside and Cameron followed.

Josie ran to her mom's room and hugged her tight. She was shaken by the noise. Cameron played it cool. He told his parents, "I only ran inside so I could take care of Josie."

He didn't want anyone to know that he was scared of the noise too.

"Josie, honey, it's okay!" Her dad said calmly. He rubbed her arm gently and smiled.

"It was probably just a dump truck or a dog or something else," he said.

"No, daddy! It was a monster!" Josie shouted.

"Josie, monsters aren't real. They are made up to scare little kids like you, but you're braver than that! Don't be afraid! " Her dad explained.

Cameron listened closely to his dad talking. He had heard that monsters weren't real too, but it was a really scary sound.

Maybe it was a monster? He thought. He felt silly for having the thought.

He wanted to be a good big brother to Josie. He wanted to protect her, even if that meant hiding his fear of the backyard monster. He had to be strong for her.

The next day, Cameron convinced Josie to go outside in the backyard again to play. Josie was hesitant, but she agreed. They brought their nets this time and caught all kinds of bugs for their castle.

The castle was filled with all kinds of bugs now! Ants, crickets, worms, and roly-polys. While Josie and Cameron were playing with their new creatures, they heard a sudden noise again.

"CRRRR—AAAACKK!" It was even louder than the last time.

This time, it was Cameron who jumped up and ran inside, leaving Josie behind. His heart was pounding and racing quickly. Josie ran in behind him crying.

"Baby, it's okay! What's the matter?" Her dad ran and picked her up to hug her tightly.

"It is a monster, dad! I really think it is!" Cameron shouted.

"Cameron! Don't scare your sister like that. There is no such thing as monsters." He said sternly and walked away, taking Josie to her room to comfort her.

Cameron was upset. He didn't believe in monsters, but this sound was like nothing he'd ever heard before and why hadn't he heard it before?

He didn't mean to scare Josie. He was only thinking of what was going on.

Cameron and Josie's mom walked into the room and saw Cameron crying.

"What's wrong, Cameron?" She sat down next to him and put her arm around his shoulder. Cameron cried softly in her arms.

"I didn't mean to scare, Josie. I'm just afraid, what if there really is a monster out there? What if it gets us while we're playing? I'm scared, mom!" Cameron said.

"Honey, it's okay, you didn't scare Josie. Monsters are scary, whether they are real or not. But I have something to tell you," she leaned in closely to whisper, "when you confront a monster, he has to go away forever."

"Really?" Cameron asked.

"What do you mean "confront"?" He asked again.

"I mean," she started, "that if you go up to the monster and you tell him to 'go away!' then he has to leave you alone!"

Cameron thought about this for a moment. That was a scary thing to do, to walk up to a monster. But he knew that he had to do it. He had to be courageous for himself and for Josie. He wanted to be a big brother that protected her. He didn't want to listen to fear.

The next morning, Josie refused to play outside. Cameron went alone. He was playing with his dirt castle, building a moat and a new tower when suddenly, he heard the noise again.

"GRRRAAAAATTT!" It roared.

Cameron jumped and began to run inside. Then, he stopped.

He froze mid-run and turned around to look at the gate. He could still hear the roaring of the monster. It was getting louder and louder.

He knew this was his moment. He had to face his fear.

He began to walk toward the gate slowly. He reached his hand out to open the gate.

His eyes were shut tight. He took one step forward and shouted, "GO…… AWAY!"

Cameron opened his eyes.

"Huh?!" He said. His face was filled with confusion. In front of him, stood a big, grey air conditioning vent.

Cameron laughed to himself. *This is the monster I was afraid of? It's not a monster at all!*

He was filled with joy. Even though it wasn't a real monster, he was brave enough to face it! He had the courage that his mom told him to have and he wasn't afraid anymore!

Cameron ran inside to tell his family what he did.

"Josie, Josie!" He shouted.

"I slayed the monster for you! He's gone!" Cameron said.

Josie and Cameron walked outside.

"No, you didn't – I still hear him!" Josie said, afraid. The roaring did continue, but Cameron hadn't noticed. It wasn't scary to him anymore.

Cameron walked his little sister over to the gate to show her what he found. He wanted Josie to feel safe playing in their backyard together.

"What! That's so silly!" Josie laughed. She hugged Cameron and smiled real big.

Josie and Cameron sat down by their dirt castle and played all afternoon together until the sunset. Cameron learned that it's okay to feel afraid, but you don't have to listen to fear after all!

What I've learned from this Story

I LEARNED TO BE
COURAGEOUS AND
ALWAYS FACE ALL
MY FEARS

Hidden Star

Matthew was a smaller boy for his age. Sometimes the older boys and the taller boys would pick on him for his size. They would call him names and make fun of him.

Matthew was very insecure about his size. He wanted to be bigger so he could play sports and beat the other boys in races at playtime.

One day, when Matthew was outside with some of his friends, they decided to play basketball together.

Matthew's older brother, Joe, joined the game and a few of his friends.

Joe wasn't much older than Matthew, so everyone was about the same height except for him.

"Hey Mini Matthew!" One of Joe's friends, Bill, shouted, "pass me the ball! You can't score a thing!"

Bill ran up and stole the ball from Matthew, holding it high above his head so he couldn't reach. Joe and Bill both laughed and continued on with the game.

Matthew frowned. He didn't like to be made fun of. Was there something wrong with him? Why was he different from everyone else?

In addition to being small, Matthew struggled with his speech. He sometimes slurred or stuttered when he spoke. He was made fun of for this too.

"S-s-s-up Mini Matthew! Wh-h-h-at, you didn't hear Bill? He said to pass the b-b-b-all!" Rufus, Joe's other friend, said.

Matthew had enough. He loved basketball, but he hated playing with others. They never gave him a chance to even play the game with them.

Matthew left the court. He didn't want to play with bullies anymore and he was upset.

"Honey, what's wrong?" Matthew's mom asked.

"Bill and Rufus were making fun of me again. I don't like when they say stuff about my s-s-stutter or my s-s-size," Matthew mumbled.

"Matthew, remember what grandma used to say?"

"Yeah."

"Well go ahead, say it back to me," she said.

Matthew sighed and said, "Grandma always says that bullies pick on people who are special. Who often are better than they are and they just can't see it."

"That's right, Matthew. You're special! You're different from others and that's a good thing. It's nothing to be upset about or ashamed of, even if it feels that way at times," she said.

Matthew knew his mom was trying to be helpful, but what did it matter if he was special if nobody saw it but himself?

He went to bed that night feeling defeated, as usual. He wished he didn't care so much about what others thought of him.

The next morning, Matthew decided to play basketball on his own. He was shooting the ball and making every shot. His dribbling was amazing and his ball handling skills had developed a lot since the year before.

Matthew had always had talent when it came to basketball, but because he was short, no one gave him the chance to show it off. That's why he loved to just play on his court at home alone. Just him, the ball and the hoop.

As Matthew was playing, he was thinking about all the negative comments that Joe's friends had said yesterday. He was angry and hurt. He took it all out on the basketball, just running and shooting and trying to make the best of his emotions.

Suddenly, an older man walked by and stopped at Matthew's driveway.

He just stood and watched as Matthew continued to play. Then he said, "Hey, bud! You're pretty good at this aren't you?"

Matthew turned in shock. He didn't see the man there before. He was embarrassed.

"Uh, no not really. I just like it."

"What do you mean 'not really'?! I just saw you make three shots in a row! Seems pretty good to me. What's your name?" The man asked.

"Matthew," he replied.

"Well, Matthew. Can I tell you a little secret?" The man asked.

"Uh, sure," Matthew replied.

Ugh, I hope this isn't another "Grandma Lecture," he thought.

"When I was your age, I was pretty embarrassed about my abilities. I wasn't the smartest, I was taller than all the other kids and people made fun of me. But something I loved," he continued, "was art and drawing. And I was pretty good at it."

Matthew raised his eyebrow, wanting to hear more of the story.

The old man continued, "it used to bother me how often kids would laugh at me, but one day, I had enough. I stood up to them and decided that I wasn't going to let their thoughts of me define who I am or what I'm good at."

"Who cares if I was really tall? Or who cares if I wasn't the smartest? I could draw better than anyone in my grade! I was good at something, but just had to have confidence in myself. I had to believe that my abilities made me unique and my lack of something else didn't matter."

The old man pointed to Matthew's chest and said, "I think that's what you need to do, bud. You need to believe in yourself."

Matthew thought about this for a moment.

"Well what does it matter if I believe in myself if no one else does?" He asked.

"Well, Matthew. You have to believe in yourself first before anyone else can see your true talent. You have to have confidence to show off your skills in front of others so they see it too."

Matthew was taken aback by this. He had never heard anyone say that.

The next day, Joe and his friends asked Matthew to play a game of basketball with them again so they'd have an even number.

Matthew was hesitant at first, but he decided it was time to change his mindset. He said yes.

But this time, the game was different. Matthew stole the ball from Bill, he dribbled around Joe and took it to the hoop. He scored!

He did this many times during the game and Joe was amazed. So were his friends.

"Ayeee, that-a-boy, Matty!" Bill shouted, cheering him on.

Matthew grinned. He had been confident in his abilities and now they were seen! That old man was right!

Matthew learned to believe in himself and his confidence increased. People around him began to recognize Matthew for his talents and praised him. His belief sparked others to believe in him too.

What I've learned from this Story

I LEARNED TO BE
CONFIDENT AND TO
BELIEVE ALWAYS IN
MYSELF

You've Got a Friend In Me

Judge Elementary was an all-boys school known for its little league baseball team. Everyone in the fifth-grade class had to be on the team, but the most popular boys at Judge Elementary were the stars of the team.

They were the ones who played the best and had the most talent.

Rocco was on the little league team and he was the first hitter, which meant he was really good.

Jason on the other hand was the last hitter on the team. This meant that he was not a very good player.

There were only 15 boys in the fifth grade. This meant that all the boys were pretty good friends, but typically there were two groups that formed.

One group was the first half hitter and the other was the second half. In other words, the popular and the not-so-popular.

Rocco was in the popular group. He hung out with all the other good hitters and players who were starters on the team. Rocco was different than the rest of the popular kids though.

Rocco was kind and inclusive of others. He didn't bully others, instead, he stopped bullies.

He didn't like to see other kids be sad and he didn't like to see others be mean. Rocco was a sort of hero to the not-so-popular kids in school.

Jason was one of the kids who was bullied often. Jason was smaller for his age and other kids made fun of him for it. He didn't want to make anyone mad, so he just let others say whatever they wanted, even if it hurt his feelings sometimes.

One day, Jason was walking in the hallway and a mean boy came up and smacked his books out of his arms. They fell to the floor and scattered.

Rocco saw what happened. He ran over to Jason and began to help him pick up his books.

"Oh, thanks, but I got it," Jason said, looking down at the floor.

"Nah, man. Let me help you —"

"I said, I got it," Jason said firmly. He walked off.

Rocco's feelings were a bit hurt. He didn't understand why Jason didn't want his help.

Meanwhile, Jason was just frustrated. He didn't want help because he didn't want anyone to see how upset he was. He was tired of getting picked on.

He was tired of being bullied and of never standing up for himself.

For the next few days, the bullying continued even worse. Jason thinks the mean kids could see his anger and wanted to frustrate him even more.

Every day when Jason opened his locker, some kid would run by and knock his books out of his hands again. It was upsetting.

Rocco watched every day and wanted to help Jason, but he didn't want to upset him even more.

At the end of the week, one of the mean kids knocked the books as usual, but also pushed Jason down this time.

"Hey!" Rocco shouted at the boy.

He ran over to Jason to help him up.

"I'm fine —" Jason began.

"No, let me help you. You don't deserve to be treated like this," Rocco said.

Jason grabbed Rocco's outstretched hand. Rocco pulled him to his feet and smiled.

"Let me be a friend to you, bud," Rocco said.

"I'm sorry for before. I was frustrated, but I appreciate the help," Jason replied.

Rocco walked with Jason home, as they lived close to each other.

They'd always been neighbors, but they didn't ever cross paths before since Rocco had baseball practice after school.

Rocco decided to skip it today though. He wanted to make sure those mean kids left Jason alone on his walk home.

"Seriously, thanks for sticking up for me," Jason said.

"No problem, man!" Rocco replied, "Hey, would you wanna come over and play games sometime?"

Jason was hesitant. He didn't have many friends and wasn't very good at games.

"Uh, yeah, but I'm not any good," he replied.

Rocco smiled, "That's okay! I can teach you. Wanna come today?"

"Sure!" Jason smiled and went to ask his mom. She said yes and he headed over to Rocco's to play.

Jason and Rocco became really close friends. They played together almost every day after Rocco's baseball practice.

Two unlikely friends, from different backgrounds, with different abilities. They formed a beautiful and special friendship all because of a kind act. It was a friendship the both of them would cherish forever.

What I've learned from this Story

I LEARNED THAT
FRIENDSHIP AND
FRIENDS ARE VERY
PRECIOUS

Lean On Me

Today was the day. The new NBA PlayStation game was coming out and Brock had to have it. He'd been waiting for this day for weeks!

He saved up his money some from his allowance and his parents made a deal with him that they'd pay the rest.

"Mom! Dad! We gotta go, the store opens soon!" Brock shouted.

"Hold on Brock, Dad's on the phone for work," his mom said, "we'll leave as soon as he's done."

Brock's mom walked over to the office door and whispered to his dad, "Brock's waiting, how much longer?"

Brock's dad held up his finger, showing that he would be done in about one minute.

Brock was so excited. He had butterflies in his stomach.

"Alright, bud! I'm ready! Let's go!" His dad said, walking out of his office.

They grabbed the keys and left the house, headed to the store for Brock's big day.

As soon as they arrived, there was a dreadful sign on the door.

It read: WE ARE SOLD OUT OF THE NBA GAME

Brock's face dropped. He was so upset. Tears began to fill his eyes.

"Honey, I'm so sorry! Why don't we try the other store down the street?" His mom said.

They drove down the street and there was another sign that said the same thing.

The next four stores they tried were all sold out of the NBA game that Brock so badly wanted. He was devastated.

Brock and his parents went home and Brock went straight to his room, pouting.

He was angry with his dad for being late and thought that he could've got the game if things went differently.

He didn't want to talk to his parents. He was frustrated and disappointed.

The next day at school, Brock's friends came up to him.

"Did you get it?!"

"It's awesome!"

"It's the best game ever!"

All of the boys shouted in excitement at Brock. But they saw that Brock was sad, and they stopped.

"Oh…" one of the boys said, "did you not get it?"

"They were sold out."

"Sorry, dude."

The teacher walked into the room.

"Okay everybody, take your seats!" She said.

"Please pass your field trip permission slips forward."

Class went on and the kids learned about different animal environments that day. The upcoming field trip was to the zoo, so they had to be prepared with lots of new information.

After class, Brock left quickly. On his way out, he realized he left his pencil bag behind, so he turned back.

As he entered the room, he saw Cody, the quiet boy, walk up to the teacher and he overheard them talking.

"I'm sorry, Cody. If your parents done sign the permission slip and pay the fee, then you won't be able to go," the teacher frowned.

"But... my mom said we can't afford it," Cody said, in a quiet voice.

"I know, Cody. I'm so sorry. I —" The teacher saw Brock standing in the doorway.

"Oh, Brock! What do you need?"

"Sorry, I left my pencil bag," said Brock as he shuffled over to his desk to quickly grab it. He felt like he shouldn't have heard that conversation.

He left the room and felt sad for Cody. It wasn't fair that his family couldn't afford the field trip. It was going to be the best thing that happened in school this year!

When Brock got home, he went straight to his room and dug under his bed. He pulled out his stash of money that he'd saved up for his game.

He shoved the money in his school backpack.

The next day, Brock walked into class and didn't sit down right away. Instead, he walked up to the teacher and handed her the money.

"Brock, what's this for?" The teacher asked.

"It's for Cody. So he can go on the field trip with us!"

The teacher paused. She was hesitant, but she took the money for Cody.

"That's very nice of you, Brock. Cody will love this."

Brock smiled and sat down.

After class, he saw the teacher give Cody the good news and he looked so happy.

Brock felt a sense of thankfulness wash over him. It felt so good that he could give someone else such joy. He didn't even miss not getting the game anymore. He was thankful that he'd be able to buy it if it was at the store!

Some kids can't and that's sad. Brock was grateful for the things he had and wanted to help others as much as he could, like he did with Cody.

What I've learned from this Story

I LEARNED TO BE GRATEFUL FOR WHAT I HAVE

The Strength Within

Sam was a worried little boy. He was afraid of most things, like pets, school, making friends, loud noises, and most of all, his house basement.

The basement was straight out of one of Sam's nightmares. It was dark, creepy, loud and it was very scary to him.

Unfortunately, the basement is also where his mom did laundry. Since Sam was terrified to go down into the basement, his parents made a deal with him, that he could ask them to get his laundry for him each time. He was very thankful for that.

Although Sam was afraid most often, something that he loved to do, was to play basketball. He was on the A Team at his middle school and started as the Point Guard.

Basketball helped give him confidence and strength when he was on the court.

One day, Sam was home alone before his big game. His cousin, Mark, was going to take him to the game and his parents would meet him there.

It was one of the biggest games of the season. If they won, the team would make it to the championship next week!

When Sam was getting dressed and ready for the game, he noticed that his basketball jersey wasn't in his room.

Where is it? He thought. *We're going to be late!*

He frantically searched his drawers and closet.

C'mon, c'mon!

When suddenly, he realized where it must be.

Oh no… Thought Sam.

It's in the laundry room! I can't go in there. It's too scary down in the basement. I can't…

He tried to give himself a pep talk, but it wasn't working. He was too afraid. He knew that if he waited until Mark got there, they'd be late to the game, which meant he wouldn't get to play.

Coach had strict rules. If a player was late, it was disrespectful and they had to sit out for the game as a result.

But Sam couldn't do it. The basement was too scary and dark. He was afraid.

Mark got there and surely, they were late to the game. Sam had to sit out.

Thankfully, even without one of their best players, they won!

Yes! We're going to the championship!

Even though Sam felt bad about being late, he was pumped that he'd get to go to the playoffs with his team. He wasn't going to let anything stop him from playing next time!

A week had passed and it was time for the big game.

Mark was going to pick up Sam again, since Mom and Dad had to meet him at the game from work.

But, this time, Sam made sure to put his jersey in the drawer of his closet. Or at least, he thought he had.

Where is it?! I put it right here!

His mom had taken the jersey downstairs to wash. Sam was very upset. He could not be late for this game. He wouldn't. He would do whatever it takes.

Sam walked slowly to the basement door. He stared at the darkness in terror. He placed his foot on the first step.

One down, ten to go, he thought.

He slowly inched his way down further into the dark basement.

As he reached the bottom step, he switched the light on. It was lit, but dim. Darkness still filled the room.

Suddenly, the laundry machine went off.

BEEP BEEP BEEP BEEP....

Sam jumped. He ran back halfway up the stairs.

WAIT. I have to do this.

He turned back and inched his way back down the stairs.

He took a deep breath and closed his eyes.

As he breathed out, he opened them. The laundry machine beeping suddenly changed noises.

Okay, it's not that bad! It's just like a shot clock. I know I can do anything on the court. I can do anything here too. He thought to himself.

BEEEEP...

Okay, that's three...

BEEEP...

Two...

BEEEEEEP...

One! GO!

Sam lunged at the washer and quickly grabbed his jersey.

He ran up the stairs and collapsed on the ground in relief.

He did it! He conquered his fear of the basement!

Sam was proud of himself. He couldn't believe it! He found the strength inside of him that he'd seen on the basketball court.

He now believed that the strength would be in him all the time, even in scary moments outside of basketball!

What I've learned from this Story

I LEARNED TO HAVE
STRENGTH WITHIN
EVERY TIME I FACE
HARD THINGS

39

Henry's Watermelon Habits

Once upon a time, there was a little boy named Henry. Henry lived with his mom, dad and two little brothers.

His favorite thing to do was to be outside. He loved playing in the yard and running around, but his all time favorite thing was to go to his Papa's house!

Henry loved Papa and Papa loved Henry!

They would sit together while Papa told him all about the different plants and trees they saw. Henry wished that he would grow up to be as smart and fun as Papa was.

One night, before bedtime, Papa called Henry on the phone.

"Henry!" He said, "I got some watermelon seeds in the mail today and wondered if you might want to come by tomorrow morning and help plant them?"

"Of course I do!" Henry said.

Papa was pretty famous in his town because of his watermelons. Papa's watermelons won first place, at the fair for being the biggest and best.

"Good!" Papa said, "tell your mama to have you up here by eight o'clock and we will start after breakfast."

Henry had a hard time going to sleep that night. He was so excited to be able to help his grandfather with the watermelons. He wanted to know every secret about growing watermelons like Papa's.

The next morning, Mama didn't have to tell him twice. Henry was out of bed and dressed before Mama had even filled her coffee cup.

Papa only lived a few minutes down the road. Mama dropped Henry off right at eight o'clock.

She had to leave to watch his brothers while daddy went to work.

Breakfast was amazing! Papa had made biscuits and gravy, fresh bacon, and scrambled eggs.

"The first secret of growing the best watermelons is to feed them just the right amount of good food," Papa said as he passed Henry a plate.

"Too little and they won't grow big. Too much and the vines will grow, but the fruit won't. If we feed them the wrong thing they won't grow at all."

"You mean kinda like me?" Henry asked.

"If I don't eat enough, I won't grow strong, if I eat too much I will get a tummy ache and won't be able to have fun. If I eat junk food, I won't be as healthy?"

"Something like that," Papa smirked.

After breakfast was done and leftovers were put away, Papa put on his boots and he and Henry walked to the tool shed.

Papa's gardening tools were so clean and organized. It looks like he had barely used them.

Henry thought that was strange.

The garden wasn't big but Papa had planted so many things in it. Tomato plants, cucumbers, and squash took up three rows.

Then there were green beans and black-eyed peas. Almost every row was filled with some sort of vegetable. There was one row that had nothing in it.

"This is where we will be planting the watermelons," Papa said as he pulled a handful of seeds out of his pocket. Henry stared at the small little seeds.

"How can something so small turn into something as big as a watermelon plant, Papa?" Henry asked.

"Well, Henry, you are little now but you will be a grown up, one day," Papa explained.

"Watermelon seeds and little kids are not much different. They both need food, sunlight, and love to grow to be big and strong."

Henry and Papa worked the rest of the morning planting watermelon seeds, covering them up, and watering them.

Once they were done, they went and rested in the shade of an old pecan tree, by the house.

After they had rested, Papa gathered the tools and took them to the water spigot.

"It's time to clean the tools, Henry," Papa said as he handed Henry the rake.

Henry wanted to do something fun and this wasn't fun.

"Can we wait on cleaning the tools and go play and explore, first?" He asked

"The tools are just going to get dirty again anyway," he added.

Papa didn't get upset. He had been a boy once too!

"Henry, another reason my watermelons grow so big is that I have made a *habit* of taking care of them" Papa said.

"I clean my tools because I made a *habit* of taking care of them too!"

"What is a habit?" the little boy asked.

Papa answered, "A habit is something you do over and over again until you can't keep from doing it."

"Are habits hard to do?" Henry asked.

"Some can be, but that is just because we aren't used to doing them. You brush your teeth every morning, right?" Papa asked.

"Yes!" Henry grinned showing Papa his white teeth.

"See?"

"I do see," the old man said as he picked up the water hose. "That is a habit. Is that hard for you to do?"

"No! It's easy!" Henry laughed.

"Exactly!" Papa exclaimed, "habits are really good ways to help us take care of ourselves."

Henry thought about it for a bit and said, "Papa, I don't think I mind helping clean the tools off."

"What are other habits that I can do to take care of myself, Papa?" Henry asked as they put the tools back into the shed.

"Anything that keeps your body and mind healthy. Taking a bath, exercising, and eating right are all ways to keep your body healthy."

Papa replied as he and Henry walked back to the pecan tree.

"What about keeping my mind healthy? How do I do that? Are there mind habits?" Henry questioned.

"There sure are and you are already doing the best habit!" Papa said excitedly.

Confused by what he had just heard, Henry just sat there, looking into his grandfather's eyes.

"The greatest habit you can have is to keep learning! I would say that you are doing a pretty good job of creating that habit." Papa said.

Henry was amazed. Just being curious had formed a habit that Henry didn't know he had.

All of a sudden, he wanted to learn about everything. He wanted to make more habits that could help him take care of himself.

Henry spent the rest of the summer helping Papa tend to the watermelons. He created habits, just like Papa, and his watermelon won a first place ribbon at the fair that year.

What I've learned from this Story

I LEARNED THAT
CREATING GOOD
HABITS CAN
IMPROVE MYSELF

Band of Brothers

Franklin and Spencer were the best of brothers. Spencer was 4 years older than Franklin, but they were really close.

Franklin admired his older brother.

Spencer loved being a role model for his little brother.

Spencer was an athlete. He especially loved to play soccer.

"Hey, Franklin!" Spencer shouted from upstairs.

"What's up?" Franklin replied.

"Let's go play ball!"

Franklin and Spencer used to not get along when they were younger, but as Spencer entered high school they began to grow closer.

Now that Spencer was a senior in high school, he tried to hang out with Franklin more often.

Spencer was planning to go out of state for college, but his brother didn't know. He thought that Spencer was going to community school, but Spencer was accepted to a university last week.

Plans had changed and he didn't want to upset Franklin by telling him yet.

"C'mon, let's go outside!"

Spencer grabbed the soccer ball and they ran to the backyard.

Franklin passed the ball to Spencer.

"So, are you excited for college?" Franklin asked.

"Yeah man, I am! It'll be hard, but a great experience," Spencer replied. He was nervous talking about the subject.

He really didn't want to upset Franklin.

"Well, I'm just glad you're gonna be close to me still so we can hang out." Franklin smiled and kicked the ball back to Spencer.

Spencer paused.

I've got to tell the kid, he thought, *but it'll devastate him.*

"Uh, I actually need to tell you something about that —"

"Franklin! Spencer! Time for dinner, come inside!" Their mom shouted.

Franklin sprinted inside, forgetting that Spencer had even started his sentence.

Oh well, I'll tell him later, Spencer thought.

Spencer and Franklin's parents knew about Spencer going out of state. They also knew that Spencer hadn't told Franklin yet, so they tried not to bring the subject up.

"So, how was your day boys?" Their dad asked.

"It was good, just played games and some soccer. Being out of school is nice!" Franklin replied.

"Yeah it is! Summer has been great so far," Spencer added.

"Good! Well, Spencer you got something in the mail from —" Their mom caught herself. She almost spilled the secret about college.

Franklin could feel the tension in the room. He felt like he was the only one who didn't know what was going on.

"What is it?" Franklin asked.

"I was going to tell you —" Spencer started.

"Tell me what?"

"I got accepted to Duke this fall. I won't be going to school nearby anymore," Spencer frowned.

"What?! What are you talking about?" Franklin was very upset.

He stormed out of the room and went upstairs.

Spencer sighed. He asked to be excused from the table and followed Franklin upstairs.

He knocked on his door.

"Hey, Franklin? Can I come in?" Spencer asked timidly.

Silence followed. He knocked again.

"Go away," a quiet voice came from Franklin's room.

"C'mon, bud. Can I please come in? I just want to talk."

There was a slight pause, "fine," Franklin said.

Spencer opened the door and sat on the edge of Franklin's bed.

"I'm sorry for not telling you sooner. I just didn't want to upset you." Spencer said.

"It's fine," Franklin replied, clearly upset.

"It's just, I'm sad about it too. I'm gonna miss seeing you and playing soccer with you all the time. I'm gonna miss playing games, beating you at Smash Bros and just being close to you."

Franklin frowned. He began to tear up.

"But I want you to know that I'm not really going anywhere. I mean, yeah, I'm leaving for college, but I'm still here for you! I still will be around for holidays and some weekends to hang out. I care about you a lot, dude. I know it's hard to let go, but it's a part of life. Change is inevitable, and it's always sad, but it can be happy too. Imagine how happy you'll be when I come home! It'll make our time together more special."

Spencer put his arm around Franklin and continued, "it's hard to accept, but once you do, you'll be able to find joy in the change. I promise, it'll be good for me and you both!"

Franklin sat for a moment pondering. He knew that it was good for Spencer to go for college. He wanted him to enjoy his experience and to get to go with all his friends, but he was sad about it.

"I know it will be. I want you to go, I'm just upset and... I'm gonna miss you." Franklin said, crying.

Spencer held Franklin for a moment and they just sat there.

Weeks had passed and Franklin and Spencer continued to have the best summer ever together. Franklin had begun to accept that Spencer was leaving, and it did make him appreciate the memories more. He was still sad about it, but embracing the change made the time that they had left more special.

What I've learned from this Story

I LEARNED TO ACCEPT MYSELF JUST THE WAY I AM

A Home in Both Places

Morgan's eyes started swelling and tears ran down his face. He was saying goodbye to his dad for what felt like the last time. But it was actually just the car ride back to his mom's house, where he would be leaving in a moving truck and heading for Kansas.

That was the first and last time in Morgan's life that he cried that way. As if he were squeezing the last bit of childhood out through his eyes.

His dad sat next to him in the drivers seat. Dad knew Morgan was moving back home in a year, but nothing is ever certain. So, he cried too.

Neither of them wanted to keep driving in this direction.

Morgan watched as his father left him there and drove away in a lonely car. He then turned to face the moving truck, and in front of it were his mother, stepfather, and stepbrothers.

He had always wanted brothers, but not like this.

They were both a few years older than Morgan. And they were already used to moving around a lot due to their father being in the army. But Morgan had never left his home.

As the last few things were packed into the moving truck, Morgan took one last look inside the only home he had ever known.

Morgan then looked at his stepfather who was outside the window.

He was angry with his stepfather. *Who is this man, basically a stranger, to come and ruin everything?*

To Morgan, he was the reason his real father just drove away, feeling like they'll never see one another again.

And his stepbrothers were cold. They could not understand what Morgan was going through. They tried to be more friends than brothers.

They tried to make Morgan forget what was happening, but they failed. He still remembered the day before, when he was sitting by himself at the pond and his stepfather sat down beside him. He tried to tell Morgan it'll be alright.

He told Morgan, "Moving's not that bad. Bryce has done it a dozen times and he doesn't even care."

Morgan stood up and walked away. *How could he say that?* Morgan felt disrespected.

Morgan's stepfather just couldn't see things from his perspective.

Morgan found himself in the car as they drove off, feeling truly alone, surrounded by captors.

Finally arriving at and moving into the new house was a drag. Morgan didn't like the walls, the driveway, or the neighborhood.

It was all as much of a stranger to him as the people walking down the street, like the two little girls he saw who must've been around his age.

He was nervous to meet the local kids.

Spending the rest of the summer locked away in his new room, Morgan dreaded the first day of his new school.

Just the thought of school terrified him. It's not like he can just forget all his friends from back home.

How will he make new ones when he's the new kid and they've all known each other for years already?

The first day at Spring Valley Elementary was just for orientation. The kids would go in and meet their teachers.

Morgan's heart was pounding and his hatred for this place grew as he walked down the halls.

What he found was a normal looking classroom with not a lot of kids in it yet. The teacher sat at her desk, talking to her parents. Alone in front of him was a girl named Jeska.

He thought she was cute, but she looked unapproachable.

He felt like no one wanted him there. Behind him were two other girls, Briana and Victoria. He recognized them. The two girls walking down his street.

They were his neighbors.

Staying out of the way, Morgan tried to be invisible for the first week of school.

He ignored his classmates. He thought they would treat him like he didn't exist. But he was really only doing this to himself.

When two boys, Eidan and Austin, approached him to make friends, he was shocked. Eidan asked him to come to his birthday party.

He didn't even know Morgan.

They had never talked before then, yet here he was, talking to him like a friend. Morgan accepted and went to the birthday party.

When Morgan walked into Eidan's house, he was first greeted by Eidan and his parents. They didn't talk to him like he was a lost child.

They talked to him as if he belonged there.

Eidan told Morgan to follow him downstairs where they found several other kids from the school playing.

Jeska was there. Briana and Victoria were there. Austin was there too.

They played and they laughed. Morgan found out that Jeska was from Texas and Briana was from New York.

She would also be moving to Germany soon, so she was trying to make as many last memories with her friends as she could.

Eidan and Austin had lived there for their whole lives, but they had seen many other kids just like Morgan, Jeska, and Briana who were coming and going.

They understood what Morgan was feeling when they saw him in school. So, there he was, no longer alone and surrounded by friends.

For the next year, they laughed together, they played together, and they remembered each other as Morgan felt the time fly by.

And finally, he was on his way back to see his dad again. This time with a home in both directions.

Morgan was grateful to the kids who made him forget he was 1,200 miles away from that painful last goodbye. Morgan was glad to see the world.

What I've learned from this Story

I LEARNED TO BE
KIND EVEN TO
PEOPLE I DON'T
KNOW

Game On

Marcus was a very talented kid. He was good at sports, school and video games especially. He was known for being the best at Fortnite and MazeChase.

MazeChase was a newer game that he'd started playing. He was further ahead than everyone in his class.

This game was unique. It wasn't like any other computer game, it was difficult, yet entertaining.

The goal was to beat the 3 minute timer, to beat the maze and collect all the coins in the whole maze.

If you did all three, you beat the level, but if you missed one of those goals, then you had to start all over.

Each week, the kids at school would gather around the computer lab at recess to play. It was special because every week a new level of the game came out, which made it hard to keep up with too.

But Marcus was the best and he beat the level every time it came out. At least, he did until level 30.

Level 30 was the hardest yet. Instead of a 3 minute timer, they cut it to only 2 minutes!

This is impossible, thought Marcus.

It was time for recess and all the kids were gathered around Marcus' computer watching him play.

"C'mon, dude! You can do it!" The kids shouted.

"Yeah, man! GO, GO, GO!"

The pressure was getting to Marcus. He knew he wasn't going to get it.

He was about halfway through the maze when all of the sudden he heard, "BEEP BEEP BEEP!"

The timer was up.

"AWWW!" The class sighed. It was Marcus' third try at the game and no luck.

Recess ended and Marcus walked back to class with all the other kids.

Oh well, level 20 took me a few days, this will be no problem later, he thought to himself.

The boys in class were all talking about how difficult the level was.

Was Marcus going to be able to beat it? If he couldn't, who could?!

But Marcus wasn't discouraged.

He knew that he could do it.

A few days passed and level 30 still seemed unbeatable. There was only one more day until the next level came out, and he still hadn't completed it!

That's never happened to him before. He's never been behind in the game.

Every day in the computer lab, kids lined up to see him play. He was beginning to feel insecure about his ability to win.

He decided that he would play more at home so he could have less pressure on himself.

After school, Marcus asked his dad if he could use the family computer.

"Hey, Dad? Can I use the computer? It's for a game I'm playing that I really need to win before tomorrow. It's important," Marcus said.

His dad smiled, "Of course, Marcus. Do your thing!"

Marcus sat down in Dad's big office chair. He cracked his knuckles and began to type quickly on the computer.

He got online to MazeChase and clicked "level 30."

Marcus spent hours playing. He got so close, he was almost on track to win, but just needed a few more seconds!

It began to get frustrating.

"UGH!" He shouted.

I've got to finish this... he thought.

His mom and dad stepped into the office.

"Hey, Bud!" His dad said.

"How's it going in here?" His mom added.

Marcus kept his eyes fixed on the screen, as he was in the middle of the game.

"It's going....UGH!" He slammed his hand on the table.

"Marcus! I know it's frustrating, but you can't hit things like that." His dad said with a stern face.

"I know. I'm sorry. It's just... I need to finish this game before the next level comes out tomorrow! I've never been behind before."

"Honey, it's okay if you get behind! No one's expecting anything from you. You don't have to be the best at this game to be proud of yourself." His mom reassured him.

"I know, it's not that. It's sort of a personal goal I have. I don't want to give up until I win! I know I can do it! I just need more time and need to be quicker."

"Do you want any help? Maybe Dad could help you with the maze." Mom suggested.

"No, thank you though. I want to prove to myself that I can do this on my own. I won't give up." Marcus said firmly.

He continued to play the game.

Loss after loss, Marcus didn't quit. He took a few breaks to gather himself and eat a few snacks, but then he was back at it.

It was 8pm and almost time for Marcus to get ready for bed. He knew his time was coming to a close. He had to try one last time to meet his goal and beat the level.

Okay, here we go, he thought.

The timer began. Marcus grabbed his computer mouse and made his way through the maze, working quickly.

The time kept counting.

BEEP, BEEP – The halfway point.

Marcus had one minute left. He was exactly halfway through the maze.

C'mon, c'mon, I can do this!

Marcus rounded the corner, grabbed the last coins and had one more row to get through.

There were 10 seconds left.

Yes, yes…. YES!

BEEP, BEEP, BEEP!

The timer was up and Marcus won!

He stood up quickly in his chair with his arms raised and fists closed. He was so happy.

His parents walked by and smiled at each other.

"Good job, Marcus! That's awesome! Proud of you for not giving up."

Marcus smiled to himself. He couldn't wait to tell the kids at school. He was proud of himself and knew he could do it.

What I've learned from this Story

I LEARNED TO
NEVER GIVE UP AND
TO BE PERSEVERANT
TO ACHIEVE MY
GOALS

Made in the USA
Coppell, TX
09 November 2022

86060622R00046